Children
are a
Blessing
from God

Nyki McShane

Request for information:

P.O. Box 201583
Shaker Heights, OH 44120

caabfg@gmail.com

DEDICATION

To Mother and Father for love, values, and direction.

Nyki McShane

TABLE OF CONTENTS

CHILDREN ARE A BLESSING FROM GOD

Children are the greatest gift parents will ever receive. Imagine the joy and excitement your parents experienced when receiving the news of having a child. They may have cried with joy because they had waited a long time to experience the blessing of having children.

Are you excited when given a present? Is it wonderful to receive a surprise reward? Do you smile? The answer is yes! There is much excitement when you receive a gift. That's right! You are a forever gift from God: *Psalm 127:3 "Behold, children are a heritage from the Lord, The fruit of the womb is a reward"*.

Your parents have a relationship with God. They enjoy serving God. You are a reward! You are a gift! When parents receive a gift from God, it must be handled with instruction, care, and love.

LOVE   JOY   FOREVER

God knows children very well. He did the following:

- Fashioned you together: *Psalms 139: 13 "For You formed my inward parts; You covered me in my mother's womb".*

- Wonderfully made: *Psalms 139:14 "I will praise You, for I am fearfully and wonderfully made; Marvelous are Your works that my soul knows very well".*

- Skillfully formed you in mother's womb: *Psalms 139:15 "My frame was not hidden from You, When I was made in secret".*

- God knew you before you were formed: *Psalms 139:16 "Your eyes saw my substance, being yet unformed. And in Your book they all were written, The days fashioned for me, When as yet there were none of them".*

Everything about your development was under the care and guidance of God. For example, your immune system fights off bacteria, and your nervous system is responsible for signals throughout the body for touch, sight, smell, and more.

You spent up to nine months growing inside your mother's womb. Your parents had joy and excitement waiting for the delivery of the perfect gift. They love everything about you from your hair, eyes, and skin to your touch. God put you together perfectly and your parents received the reward.

INSTRUCTION

Instruction and discipline are required when a perfect gift such as yourself is received from God. Some instructions from parents could be difficult to obey: turn off the video game, clean your room, do your homework, turn off the iPad, put away your toys, go to bed.

You may not want to follow instructions and immediately reply, "Mommy, please! Daddy, please!" The response from your parent is probably: "No." Hearing no is sad and difficult to accept. It may feel like rejection or like you have done something wrong. You may wonder the reason to remain obedient to parents.

It's simple. You are a blessing from God.

It may seem unfair to have rules and instructions to follow and corrective action when necessary. However, it's to prepare you for the beautiful journey and obstacles you may encounter in adulthood: Hebrews 12:11 *"Now no chastening seems to be joyful for the present, but painful; nevertheless, afterward it yields the peaceable fruit of righteousness to those who have been trained by it"*.

Chastening is temporarily unpleasant, but it will have a positive impact on personal development during your childhood. Parents are placing you on the right track for good behavior. Parents know it's right for children to learn about God, receive an education, and be obedient to their parents: *Ephesians 6:1 "Children, obey your parents in the Lord, for this is right"*.

Your parents are preparing the way for you to make good decisions when you reach adulthood. When you begin to accept discipline, your relationship with your parents will improve because you are more likely to learn from your mistakes and do as your parents ask.

PARENTS LOVE THEIR CHILDREN

Believe it or not, parents love their children. Yes, it's true.

How do you know your parents love you? Your parents love you because each day they make sure you have breakfast, lunch, dinner, and maybe some sweet treats on occasion. They make sure you have clothes and shoes to wear. Don't forget about the bed to sleep in at night. Parents make sure that you take medicine when sick. Parents take you for routine doctor and dental visits. It may not be fun, but it's necessary to keep you healthy. All these things and much more are done because you are a blessing from God.

Ask your parents about the first time they held you in their arms. Ask about the first time you smiled. Ask about the joy your parents experienced as you took each bite of baby food. Ask about the first time you cried. Ask about the innocence and peace they see on your face while sleeping. Ask about the hugs and kisses and what they mean to your parents. You will see joy spread across your parents' faces.

Each day your parents spend time with you is a blessing. After all, you are a precious gift from God. Honor your father and mother for the care and love provided to you: *Ephesians 6:2 "Honor your father, and mother," which is the first commandment with promise"*.

Do your best to pay attention, follow instructions, and have good behavior. Your parents received a wonderful reward which requires great responsibility.

Always remember, you are loved and are a blessing from God.

ABOUT THE AUTHOR

Nyki McShane is very happy and honored for the opportunity to write his first book. His goal is that parents can use the key talking points and scripture references to create a further dialogue with their children, expressing care, joy, and love in the parent-child relationship.

One time, when asked, "Why is it necessary to obey your parents?" For a moment, He was puzzled by this question because, in his thoughts, only your parents should have an answer. How could he direct youth about obeying parents if cultures may be different, lifestyle, etc.? But then he realized there is a common thread that everyone can all hold onto.

Using his childhood experience in developing a foundation, he found the answer to this question. Being an advocate for youth and young adults is his passion. Also, he loves to encourage and inspire youth and young adults to be the very best for God and engage with them so that their talents shine brightly.

Their voice should be heard, and he wants to promote their spiritual growth along with seeking personal desires to enrich their lives.